Stingrays

A Collection of Poetry & Prose

by

Carlos Harleaux

STINGRAYS

Copyright ©2017 by Carlos Harleaux.

Published by 7th Sign Publishing

(www.PeauxeticExpressions.com)

All rights reserved. No part of this book may be reproduced or transmitted in any form or by any means without written permission from the author/and or publisher.

ISBN 978-0-692-79646-7

Book Cover Design and Illustrations by Michael Lamb

Photography by Renato Rimach

My Gratitude

First and foremost, I have to thank God. I'm truly blessed that He has given me the opportunity to present my fifth book with to. I don't take for granted the allowance He has given me to have a creative outlet for all of the many random thoughts floating in my head!

My parents, Debra and Ronnie Swisher and Carl Harleaux, are the biggest encouragers I could ever ask for. I love you and I'm forever grateful for you.

My wife, Alexandria Harleaux, has always remained very patient, loving and supportive throughout this entire process. I love you.

John Patrick Adams, the first author to believe in 7th Sign Publishing. Thanks so much for your tremendous support brother since day one. Shirley Thomas, I'm pleased you chose 7th Sign to share your "Introduction" with everyone.

Also, for all of my friends and family who have believed in my dreams, without prompting. I may not have said enough in the past, but each of you having my back gives me the energy to keep moving.

Special thanks to Michael Lamb for the awesome cover art you created for me! Renato Rimach, thanks to you as well for the great photography!

Anyone who has ever purchased any of my previous books, reposted my blogs, watched my review videos or shared how my writing has touched them, thank you!

If I failed to mention anyone, please blame it on my head and not my heart.

My sincere hope is that this book is as much of a therapeutic and thought-provoking read as it was for me in creating it.

I dedicate *Stingrays* to the memory of my uncle, Rodney Swisher. Uncle Rodney, you had one of the purest hearts of anyone I have ever met. I know you are smiling even brighter in heaven than you did here on earth. You will always be in my heart and my thoughts. For now, I'll just find comfort in looking up and finding your "smile in the sky" ☺.

Gratitude With A Kick

The greatest victories are never won alone. I decided to do something that I had never seen done before with the release of *Stingrays*. I knew that I was going to release the book in digital form. However, I thought I would give people a chance to get a physical copy as well. These amazing individuals believed in this unorthodox vision enough to invest in print copies of the book before the official release of the ebook (released on my birthday, February 4th, 2017).

I would like to give a very special thanks to John Patrick Adams, Tammie Henry, William Belcher, Brian S Ference, Bill Hargenrader, Andre Wallace, Helmut Schindlwick, Shana Lee Dixon, Debra Harleaux Swisher, Ronnie Swisher, Margaret St. John, LaWanda Evans, Cecelia Tanner, Runette Harris, Carla Harleaux Gonzalez, Dina Howard, Alicia Dickerson, Maggie Lois West, Carl Harleaux, Gloria Hatcher-Gonzalez and Tambria Barnes! Plus, thank you to everyone who contributed towards the Kickstarter.

I sincerely hope that more authors find creative ways such as Kickstarter to release their books. This is the wave of the future and I am forever grateful to those who dared to see the vision with me!

The Initial Sting (Introduction)

I have always been a lover of water. Water is one of God's most soothing and interesting creations, especially when we think about waters of the ocean. Every book I have ever written has to start off with the concept and title first. The title and concept are part of the back bone of how I am able to write.

I remember having the idea to release another poetry book a little over a year ago. I was browsing the internet, when I kept seeing a pop up about stingrays on the computer. I had no idea why images of stingrays kept popping up on my computer. I hadn't even searched for anything close to that online before then. The pictures of the various stingrays almost seemed to haunt me and that's when it hit me – *Stingrays*.

I started researching more about these very interesting and odd looking fish. For the most part, they are harmless and mind their own business in different parts of the seafloor. They can easily camouflage with their surroundings, taking on different colors. Many of them grow over 6 feet long and can weigh almost 800 pounds. Plus, ancient dentists even used the venom from the stingray's spine as an anesthetic.

Life makes it easy to feel "stung" by certain things, even when we feel like we are minding our own business. We all react to life in different ways, depending on our environment, influence of those around us and our own personal beliefs. *Stingrays* details my feelings about certain situations, whether it's the familiar pursuit for financial gain, matters of the heart or the impact of social media on self-esteem. My desire is that you feel the sting of passion put into this work and use it to enhance your life in some way.

Table of Contents

The Initial Sting (Introduction)	6
Between the Sheets	11
Loose Lips	13
I Remember	15
Fault Lines	17
Pink Velvet	18
Soul Food	19
Eye Candy (Essay)	21
Feed Me Ratchet	23
Armor Peace	24
Big Buts	25
Guns and Roses	26
Time To Stay Woke (Essay)	28
Nothing Is Sacred	30
Surround Sound	32
Twenty-Something	34
What Happens In Love	35
Mr. Justify	36
No Shade	37
First Impression	38
Dirty Mirrors (Essay)	39
I'm Not Ready To Forgive You	41
Stab In The Dark	42
Permission	43
Chat Talk	44
Who Are You Following? (Essay)	45

Mine Hurts More	47
Poor Potential	48
Six Figures	49
Poetry Is Not Dead	52
Now Trending	54
Lies and Lullabies	55
Wondering Eyes	57
Get Down To Come Up (Essay)	58
Breathe	60
Enabler	62
Rinse.Wash.Repeat.	63
Homesick	65
Awake	66
I Heard About You (Essay)	68
Incapable	70
Green Fiends	72
My Current Situation	73
Glutinous Monster	74
Bed Warmer	75
Kissy Face	77
When The Dam Breaks (Essay)	78
Whispers	80
Marked Up	81
If These Chairs Could Talk	83
It's Gonna Burn	85
Sniff	87
Quicksand (Don't Pull Me Out)	88

Keep Digging If You Want To (Essay)	89
You Get What You Don't Ask For (Essay)	91
Seashells	93
Freedom To Think (Don't Speak) – Essay	94
Make Me A Believer	96
Proof In The Negatives	98
Skin Deep	99
Tangible Lucidness	100
Smile In The Sky	101
No Cream In The Middle (excerpt)	102

Between the Sheets

Turn the sheets back
So I can see you better
So I can inhale you deeper
Skin to skin
And witness your glorious splendor
Leave the lights on
The experience is more memorable that way
Besides, I'd hate to feel my way
Around such a rousing beauty
In the pitfalls of darkness
Tell me all your thoughts
Whisper your fantasies into my ear
I'll keep them quietly sequestered
Take control when I ask you to
Bite my lips, pull my hair, whip me while
You tie me up in this velvet chair
Never set me free and offer me
Decadent, incredible edibles
But don't forget to be gentle when
You know I need it most
Leave your inhibitions on the coat rack
If you play nice, I might let you
Have them back when I'm done
Giving you an experience that's too spectacular
For virtual existence,
An astringent lifting and sifting
The surface, shallow preconceived notions
From your brain
What's behind door #1
You're not afraid to go deeper are you?
Don't tell me you're scared

To get a little messy, are you?
Drop your tepidness to the floor
Follow me down the hazy corridor
When it's all said and done
They'll want to know just how
The creamy center oozed
And spilled to the floor
Just tell them
They should have been there

Loose Lips

Loose lips let slip
What is fiction
What is truth
Loose lips lie and say
This only stays between me and you
Loose lips always seem to
Leave the latch off the door to trust
Listening is not their forte
Because always speaking out of turn
Is an absolute must
Loose lips will have you feeling confused
Thinking you said what you know
You really didn't say
Freedom of speech, clearly abused
Loose lips lock the hearts of those
Who yearn to be transparent
They slither their writhing tongues
Spreading anything and everything
That keeps their lips occupied and relevant
What would happen if one day
We did away with all the loose lips
Lessened the vice grip of
Meaningless exchanges of communication
Just might cease
There'd be more love in homes
And less violence in the streets
More understanding
Less judgment
Making room for respect
To the respective vantage points
We all have a voice

And a mouth with which to speak
But sometimes loose lips
Just need to shut the hell up
And let still silence take the lead

I Remember

If I try with all my might
Squeeze my eyes really tight
Block out all the white noise
And turn down all the lights
I remember, yes I do
I can recall how it felt
To be atop the mountain's peak
Before the great fall
You were some kind of special
But that was so many moons, stars, leaps, bounds
And showers ago
Over time, I've washed away
Every trickling, creeping, seeping, leaking
Thought of you
Down the drain
I don't mean to put it so bluntly
But I must have been out of my mind
Desperately digging out of a rut
So deep it must have kissed Earth's crust
Alright, ok if I must admit it
It was love, I think
Maybe so, I don't know
Nevertheless, I thank God
For the beautiful gift
Of the present
Without it, I couldn't call you the past
If I try with all my might
Squeeze my eyes really tight
Power down the sounds of sanity
And turn off all the lights
I can honestly say

I do remember what we were
But from this clear vantage point
Today, it all just seems like a blur

Fault Lines

Is it you or is it me?
Is it them or is it we?
The ground is shaking
Quaking beneath us
Causing us to lose
The little bit of equilibrium
We once held on so firmly to
Tip toeing on eggshells
Hoping we don't break the backs
Of promises we prayed to keep

Pink Velvet

These walls were once plush
Rushing with streams of succulent waters
Butterflies bickered just to get to be
The first to rest their wings atop the morning dew
But that was once upon a time
That was once, short lived, before
The frequent friction and a-dick-tion
Changed the corridors
And diction of pink velvet so warm
Like healing honey on a wound cut
From life's sundry thorns
Now, there is literal and figurative evidence
Of being tattered and worn
You thought hell hath no fury like a
Woman scorned, so you flipped and turned
And twerked and burned and then medicated
Just to learn that the velvet you once possessed
So pretty, so sweet, so beautiful, so regal
Is now nothing more than a mere remnant
Of yesteryear's glory
What ever became of the pink velvet woman?
Does she even exist anymore?

Soul Food

I'm still here waiting
With knife and fork
For my hot plate
My lower extremities are getting stiff
And at this rate
By the time it gets here
I'll be old and gray
No more salty sweets, fried treats
Popcorn bites and colorful buzzed drinks
I want some soul food
That stick to my ribs food
The kind that makes me sleepy
So I have to take a nap afterwards food
I've unfolded my napkin and
Placed it in my lap
As the images surround me
Tornadoes compromised of scantily clad
Camera shots and thirst traps
I used to fall for those
Before I grew up, became wise
Put those childish things aside
Don't get me wrong
My eyes can't deny such a
Flesh induced high
Having me weak in the knees
Singing my, my, my
But how can one really survive on
Crispy, crunchy, savory, juicy, moist,
Finger licking good, slap yourself sweet
Toes curling in my seat....appetizers?
I'm getting impatient

And I don't think my desires
Are too much to ask
There is more to life than
A basketball wife, with a soccer ball ass, right?
Yet social media and every time I turn on the TV
Would have me believe
This is all there is to achieve
All that I should dream
So, yes I see you
Packaged in your bright, shiny wrapper
Waiting to be undressed
But I need something that will last

Eye Candy

Our current society is one of microwave attention spans. As social media continues to evolve and turn into even more of the beautiful monster than it is, many people only look for quick thrills. What better way to get attention than to exploit yourself online. The "Sniff" and "Soul Food" poems you just read touch on this notion, particularly when it comes to women. I always find it funny when I hear women say, "You have no right to treat me like a hoe, just because I'm dressed like this". Well....

We teach people how to treat us and I don't care how progressive we have become, some things never change. Many women don't realize the sexiest woman in the room is not necessarily the one who wears the most revealing outfit. Sure, she may be good for a good night or two, but that's about it. The woman who really holds the power is the one who looks better than all of the women in the room, but leaves something to the imagination. However, it seems imaginations are a thing of the past. Don't get me wrong. There is something for everyone and everyone loves a great piece of eye candy, be it male or female. Don't trust anyone who tells you otherwise, because they are probably a liar.

Entertainers and celebrities are often blamed for being the negative influence for people exploiting themselves. There can be some blame placed for the inundation of cheap sex that is targeted at both women and men. At some point, we have to be accountable for our own actions though. Famous people who portray a certain image are getting paid for it.

The average person on the street taking on some of those same personas isn't getting anything in return but a tarnished reputation. No one can survive on eye candy forever.

Feed Me Ratchet

Don't feed me your intellect and multi-cultural dialect
I'd rather crawl around down here
With the lowly insects, roaches,
Rocking my Michael Kors, Givenchy and occasionally Coaches
The flyest piece of @#$$ that is
Not even dignified enough for flies to land on
I'm salivating for your confusion, misuse and overt abuse
Pass the cup to you and now you have the juice
Let's not call a truce and keep this civil warfare going
Never dodging formations of conformity
But rather smashing right into them
Pockets turned inside out, lights out
But when the lights come on, my broke @ss is
Ready for the show
I'm on the front row, stunting until I can barely stand
And eventually fall to the floor
Some say I did for the Vine
But it's just a matter of time before
You follow the slop and slime left in my footprints

Armor Peace

When you feel like you can't muster
The strength to master their defeat
I'll be your guiding light and cool compress
In times of extreme heat
I won't let you be their casualty
I'll be your breast plate to
Protect your heart from their daggers
Be your helmet to encompass your mind
In a safe haven so sublime
You'll fly sky high above the battlefield
And when we encounter turbulence,
I'll be your trusted pilot
Bringing you in for a safe landing
Together we could win
If you would just
Let me be your armor peace

Big Buts

Get your big but out of my face
It has blocked my view for far too long
And while you're at it
Take your ifs, doubts and maybes with you
Believing in your buts just
Blocked me from my destiny
I won't be the one to say
Your big but got the best of me

Guns and Roses

Another clip is emptied as
Broken glass and blood
Coagulate next to each other
On the pavement
Years later the stains still remain
As another mother cries
Pools of grief and agony all over the petals
So delicately laid over the casket
All because someone so carelessly took his life
All because someone carelessly disregarded that
She was worthwhile enough to live
His hopes and dreams
Are now painted on murals
As we are left to remember her smile
More bullets fly with no respect
Of person, creed, gender or orientation
Is this the the core belief of our nation?
Waiting in the shadows ready to shoot em up
And kill a mockingbird and everything
That has breath and was once caged, but now free
Guns have now united with roses
In unholy matrimony
And we do solemnly swear to bear witness
To the exchange of the rings and things
That perpetually tie these two together forever
You may now kiss life as you know it goodbye
Because it can all be gone in the blink of an eye
So we keep roses on hand thinking
They will somehow soothe the burning hearts of men
And women left to remember
They won't

The roses are meant to represent a beautiful
Replica of life
But they don't
Not when they fail to bring resurrection
Besides there aren't enough roses to go round
For all these casualties we see
And the ones hidden from view
Alterations of the fabric of truth
If anyone else sees why these two should
Not be joined together forever
Repeat after me, let no man put asunder
And say I do

Time To Stay Woke

Are you woke? Do you know what it takes to stay woke? Basically, are you paying attention?

In case you haven't heard of the term "stay woke", it means to pay attention to what's going on around you. Lately, more than ever, the world has been forced to sit up and take notice about issues concerning religion, race, gender and sexual preference. Virtually no stone (or person) has been left unturned. As a result of these stressful, heinous and catastrophic events, there is a heightened sense to read between the lines for the things that are right under our noses.

There is a certain social awareness that I believe everyone should have. Life has a way of making us become more aware (and at times tolerable/intolerable) of our surroundings in its own time. However, I do have an issue with people who turn every conversation, opportunity, news headline and constellation in the sky as sign to "stay woke". What constitutes being able to "stay woke"?

The bottom line is people will choose what fits best into their lifestyle. People make excuses for the demons they are wrestling, but have the audacity to criticize someone else for how they handle theirs. Let's be clear and realize that spending hundreds of dollars of at the bar and then standing on top of a soap box preaching economic empowerment is not staying woke. That's just frivolously throwing away money. Choosing who will be assisted in times of need, while blatantly ignoring others in the same situation is not staying woke. Promoting unity on social media but gossiping about every associate, friend or foe is not staying woke.

Somebody let me know when it's really time to wake up.

Nothing Is Sacred

Whatever happened to the days
When pinky swears sealed the deal?
Or when you could sleep soundly
On the security of a scout's honor
What about when a round of thumb wars
Was all you needed to call a truce?
When the only complications we had
Were not letting the sherbet from Push Pops
Melt and drip through the tube
When commitment wasn't measured by
Online impressions or being included on a guest list
But a simple yes or no was circled
And we dreaded being
Stuck in that maybe box, just like too many
Peanut butter and jelly sandwiches
Sticking firmly to the roof of our mouths
Don't you remember when it was actually safe
To play outside after the street lights dimmed?
And drive-bys and hate crimes
Were mostly what we saw on primetime films
When pushing the envelope was
Guys wearing backwards pants and
Girls with their hats to the back
With their pants down low
And sexy could be found standing
Inside of a pair of overalls, fully clothed
Instead I am frozen solid
Tapping on the glass
Stuck in this horrific time capsule
Wishing for back-to-the-future's past
And we ask, how long will the dissention last?

If anyone finds a way to get back
To when something as simple as
Removing the plastic from a CD
And reading the liner notes was sacred
Beam me up and tell me how to get there fast

Surround Sound

When I put these headphones on
It's you and I
In our private galaxy
Suspended in the sky
Feeling the bass thump rhythmically
Through my chest like we do
And the strings glide effortlessly
Just like us too
The pulsating, melodic
Keys of the piano
Like the ones that unlock
You to me
We forgot to come up for air
When the thunderous rolls of the tympanis
Imitate our race to see
Who will finish first
Fully immersed underneath the sax waves
We held our breaths so long
We swam right past the interludes
I knew you would feel so robust
Just like trumpets, trombones and tubas
That hold engaging conversations
Within these four walls
So caught up, wound up
Gotta find a way to release
This pent up aggression
If every good boy really does fine
Then why must I find myself
Standing here alone
When the last note of the song
Dissipates into the atmosphere

You're nowhere to be found
Maybe next time you'll join me
And we can reconnect, re-emerge
And submerge in the confines of
This surround sound.

Twenty-Something

I gave you the most vibrant years
Of my life
Waited on your mark, set, go
Watched opportunities pass me by
Whisked away with fair weather winds blown
You gave me a promise of a promise
Strung me along just long enough
To drain me of my youth
The audacity to try to trick me
Your tactics are so uncouth
Naïve and unknowing
I didn't think there was better
So I stayed strapped in for worse
Watched my joy slow creep away
Like a hearse in a funeral procession
Back to life, back to reality
No matter how I tried
Nothing seemed to resuscitate the inner me
This was supposed to be my
Time to shine
My time to thrive
But I couldn't see which road to take
For all the dirt kicked in my eyes
But don't bring me your balloons, streamers
Cards and confetti for my pitty party
Because this is just a mere
Recounting of a hard lesson learned
That finding the strength to leave you
Was a Godsend
I've got my mojo back and
I'm feeling like a twenty-something all over again

What Happens In Love

Whatever happened to keeping your mouth closed
And waiting until things boiled over before you
Called that one friend that has to hear your breakup story
Again and again for the fiftieth time
It's yet another lie
Since when were relationships that consisted
Of more than two cool
Exponentially entertaining fools from
Friend lists that we barely even know
Let alone even like
Oh just posted another pic
It's date night out
See, we're fine
No worries no strife
This crap shoot for love is
Complicated and quirky enough
Without all these intoxicating distractions
Infractions on singular and joint beliefs
There's no relief or rest for the weary
For those that walk around
Void of poker faces
When the chips are down
Perhaps a winning draw will
Serve as a reminder that
What happens in love....
Stays in love

Mr. Justify

Hello, it's me again
I don't mean to bother you
Or take up too much of your time
But I've gotten myself tangled up
Caught up in a mess I can't undo again
In a bind, slave to my mind
And need your help because
I've abused the truth
Maybe told more than my share
Of a few white lies
Broken a few hearts
And caused several sets of eyes to cry
I don't know why I keep
Leaving these loose ends untied
But Mr. Justify
I always heard you could restore
Sight to the blind
Even if it's nothing more than
False hope you supply
Oh please, Mr. Justify
I need your advice
It cuts too deeply to face
The truth of these vices
So help me live another lie
Thanks in advance
I'll be here awaiting your reply on stand by

No Shade

If you feel that cool breeze
Resting on your shoulders
Feeling like someone's behind you
Breathing down your back
Don't mind the branches
Brushing against your neck
And those leaves whirling
Around your ankles
If the bark starts to bow
And break from leaning in your direction
Don't mind that
It's just the portent of my exit
If the vultures start to swarm in circles
High above the sky
Swooping down low
And the grass ceases to grow
Really, it's not your fault
When the dust starts to rise
And walk inside your eyes
Don't cry
Really, it's ok
No shade
It's just karma paying you a visit

First Impression

Does my vernacular vivaciously astound you?
Make you lose footing on the shallow ground you stand on?
Does my polished image, without a blemish
Leave you probable cause to believe there's something hidden
Something missing and more than meets the eye
See I don't know how it feels to walk in your shoes
And neither you in mine
Yet something tells me if you slipped your feet inside
You wouldn't last long enough to get your shoes tied
So catch your grip and fix your face
I am where I am supposed to be
And not out of place
I am here
Unraveled, unshaken, unbreakable
I am here
Unbeknownst to you, I always was
Always will be
I can't help the fact that you
Just decided to deem me worthy
Of expressing my own being
Inside my own skin
Impressed, are you?
Well I am thrilled to know
You can finally see
What was right in front of you all along

Dirty Mirrors

Do you remember what life was like before selfies? I know, it seems like many moons ago. In today's society, we have become so accustomed to taking pictures of ourselves and have even created devices (the selfie stick) to take the best pictures possible. Even if you don't participate in the selfie craze, chances are you know someone who does. One of my biggest pet peeves is when people take pictures in front of dirty mirrors.

For some, it's not enough that their mirrors are literally caked with toothpaste, water, makeup and soap. There are also some people who think it's totally acceptable to have their pile of clothes (let's pray they're at least clean) on the floor behind them in the bedroom. Who does that? Unfortunately, way too many people.

Just like those dirty mirrors that distract us from the pictures we want people to see, our lives function the same way. No matter how much we dress up on the outside, what's ugly in the background (jealousy, hate, lack of forgiveness, etc) eventually makes its way up to the forefront. We can push those things like money in the bank, an expensive car or beautiful physical attributes to center stage all day long. In fact, there's nothing wrong with that if that is what you truly find most valuable in life. However, those unpleasant things we choose not to showcase have a way of stealing the spotlight.

So what type of reflections are your projecting for others to see? Are your mirrors clear and fully representative of the images you want people to know you by? Or are the background elements of your life causing everyone else to lose focus on what your purpose truly is. Dirty mirrors? Maybe it's time to clean them up.

I'm Not Ready To Forgive You

Perhaps tomorrow when the sun rises
I will be ready to part my lips and utter
Some sort of subtle semblance of a truce
You know I'm never wrong and you're hardly right
But I can't let you know
So I'll keep up the fight
Although my mind is soothed
Although the fire in my chest has cooled
I can't let you know that your smile
Has made me forget what I was
Even so angry about to begin with
I can't let it show that
The real reason I'm upset has nothing
To do with you
But that one remark was the last
Piece of bark from the tree of anger
That had been rising up in me all day
And it all yelled timber at the wrong time
So all of my frustrations unfortunately fell on you
I know it's not right
Know it's not ok
And I'll forgive you I will
In my own time
In my own way
I'm just not ready to go through with it today

Stab In The Dark

Let's play a game of
Hide and seek
To find what once was
The manifestation of my dreams
Now I'm somewhere suspended
Hanging by a momentary thread, in between
Two sides of a story that never
Seem to gel
Oh well, what the hell
The blinding bliss
Is nothing but a mere flicker
Until poof, lights out
Just like that
Our equilibrium is thrown off
May be too late to get it back
My love is cold
My love is hiding
My love is timid
No longer bold
Catch me if you can
Take a stab in the dark
Capture it if you dare
Like a thief in the night

Permission

Bomp bomp bomp bomp
It can't be morning already
Look at my phone to find
I'm late already
Ease out of the bed slow and steady
For a brief moment of medication
Without hesitation I scroll through
Notifications, posts and emails
That immediately remind me
I just may not be tall enough
My shoulders might be a couple inches shy
of being broad enough
My pockets aren't deep enough and
Dare I say it, my popularity index indicates
I may not be worth enough
That's tough
This trough of wading
For the approval of society
Is getting sloshy
Subservient to live beneath
My unalienable rights
This is my land, but I have to ask
For refuge to get rest at night
Hoping I won't be refused this time
Please, May I and Thank You
Might just be polite
The water has risen to my chest
Now it salutes me at my eyes
I don't advise, I still need your permission
to stay afloat
Do I?

Chat Talk

Today I had the best conversation ever
Yet I never heard inflections
Echoed from vocal chords
Or the kind of guttural laughter
That makes you forget
All your pain
Wait
Is it time to go already?
I'm logging off now but
I'll chat with you tomorrow

Who Are You Following?

I think it's safe to say we've all had that moment when we realize we have added the wrong person on social media. Perhaps the person turned out to be a stalker or just simply posted much more than you cared to see come across your news feed. This has definitely happened to me more times than I care to admit. However, there is one person that I followed on Instagram that has since stuck out in my mind.

The person was a guy who followed me first. Before I decided to follow him back, I looked through his pictures and read his bio. He seemed normal enough (whatever that means). His page consisted of meal prep examples, time with his children, workout tips and inspirational quotes.

Then one day I saw a meme that popped up on my home page, which just happened to be from his account. The meme was a cat stretching its limbs and yawning. The caption over it read, "Me knowing I don't have to get up for church on Sunday morning because I'm an atheist". I'm a Christian and this immediately raised an eyebrow with me. I must admit though that I did not unfollow him immediately. In fact, I didn't unfollow him until two days later. Some of you may be wondering why it took me so long to unfollow him in the first place. Believe me, I get it and asked myself the same question.

How many times have you seen someone who professed to be Christian (or any other religion) and their posts are in total opposition to their beliefs? Did you lose count yet?

Yes, I did too. Don't get me wrong. We should stand firm on our beliefs, while remembering to respect those who have other beliefs. Somewhere along the way, many of us failed to respect ourselves enough to at least not make public what is in direct conflict with who we say we are.

Mine Hurts More

So which ones hurt the most?
Is it the ones that sting and burn
When the sunlight peels back
Our eyelids in the morning
Or the ones that reek of a stench
That fills every crack and crevice
Stomping through the concrete
Bigger than the elephant in the room
That has demolished all of the walls
Walking on a tight rope of fact or fiction
Some can be told and processed
So eloquently that to believe them is gospel
And refuting them must mean blasphemy
Are the deceitful lacerations that draw the most blood
The ones where we already saw the danger coming
Like blinking yellow caution lights
Or that dump girl that seems to run
Smack dab into the arms of her killer in those
Predictable horror films
It's a nightmare, quite a scare
That we have been tied in and to
Have our greatest fears been confirmed?
Does the discomfort make us scream, kick
Claw and squirm?
We never seem to learn
That they all eventually sting and burn
So let's not use them at all, shall we?
Who are we kidding?
Long live the lie and if
You agree, throw your hands up high

Poor Potential

Ah yes, that familiar scenario
Has reared its hopeful head
Yet again
It's the same song and dance
And questionable pomp
And circumstance
To hear you, see you, feel you
Cry and weep
With your head hanging low
As you keep reassuring me
Of things that haven't come close
To fruition, yet I'm supposed to believe
Yet I'm supposed to give you some
Kind of reprieve
When the relief would be when
Your actions become congruent with your promises
Yes, please don't make them
If you have no intentions of meeting them
If you have no intentions of nurturing them
And watering them from their infancy
Seedling stage to a full grown tree
You see, potential was cool for a while
Potential kept the inevitable at bay….for a while
But I can no longer stand on the shaky, uneven
Crumbling ground of such said things
That are only said, never being.

Six Figures

As I look in the mirror
I don't recognize me anymore
Listening to those I claimed as mi amor
Brought me to this very moment
Of face fillers, lip plumpers, breast augmentations
And reconstructive lacerations
They all unanimously said at different times
That I wasn't pretty enough
So I figured I'd prove them all wrong
Show them just how beautiful I could be

I broke many hearts
Though it was never my intention
Well, maybe I shouldn't mention the fact
That I was, scratch that
I am a nympho
In doors, outdoors, back seats, presidential suites
Where I went, they followed
I filled them up and left them hollow
I figured this must be the life
Get them all, squeeze them tight
Then send them home
Before the end of the night

I worked until my joints ached
Kissed enough butt until
My breath stank
I drank the fast track potion
As they tugged at my legs
Begging me to pay attention to them
They pleaded, but only for so long

Now that the pleading has ended
I am all alone
Now they have their own
Coat tail pullers
I figured the climb would pay off
But it just left me atop the mountain, alone

I was a victim whose story
They never wanted to listen to
So I grabbed their attention by the throat
And watched them gasp and struggle to catch
Their breath
Just like I did
I only let go when the whites
Of their eyes
The red flushed fear
In their skin
And blue, oxygen deprived lips
Comprised my version
Of the Amercian dream
I figured they needed to see
How I suffered, first hand
Oops, I didn't mean to take
The life of another man

I am waiting with
My palms open momentarily
And fists closed for
What feels like an eternity
Closed mouths don't get fed
So mine stays open uttering
All the request my heart desires
Until my mouth becomes so dry

You could strike a match inside
The fire that boils and bubbles
Beneath me
How could they and not have I?
I figured making my petition known
Was the only way to live my life

I collected every piece of literature
I could get my hands on
And a handful of graduation ceremonies
That certified me as an educated professional
I was the go-to for the Who's Who
And to this day never me
One who can contest my intellect
Or has such a wide range of dialect
But when you dissect beyond
The sophisticated exoskeleton
There is an empty being
I figured being the smartest at the table
Would ensure my place as a quintessential staple
All it did was help me more accurately
Pontificate how wrong I was
About my identity
Or the lack thereof

Poetry Is Not Dead

If I had just a nickel
For every fickle opinion
That has escaped the lips
Of those who try to dissect
And dictate my flow
I'd be rich
I don't need a palm reader
To tell me what they're going to say
Before their mouths speak it
Is poetry really profitable?
You know that's a hard market
And I know you love your art but
Aren't you doing this for money?
Now that's not the kind of the thing
You should really say
If you want to be considered
One of the great poets of today
Your rhyme and reason
Has to weave in and out
Of every eb and flow
And change with the seasons
Give people what they want to hear
That's how they do it on the reality shows
There's nothing wrong with some spicy
Housewives and hoes every now and then
Is there?
There's nothing wrong with mixing in
A few white lies to alter the color
Of your truth, is there?
I say, I don't know but
You tell me

Here's a pen and paper
To write all you see
Inside your mind's eye about me
And what I should be
To be more alive, awakened
Be more astute
Be more connected
Do what everyone wants me to
But that wouldn't be poetry
Far away from what we would claim
It would then just be conformed
To another mere form of entertainment
Poetry, on our terms
Based on our memories, heartaches, victories and recipes
Served hot, fresh and ready for
Our minds to masticate
Is never ever dead

Now Trending

#Somehave exposed extremities
#Somehave stood up for their truth at all costs
#Somehave lied and finagled their way to the top
#Somehave risen above the filth
To become the cream of the crop
#Somehave died and can't even witness their impact
#Somehave blessed us with their words of encouragement
#Somehave shaken their heads in disbelief
Wondering how in the hell they got there in the first place

Lies and Lullabies

Now I lay me down to sleep
If I should die, before I wake
I pray the Lord my soul to take
And hope no one is slain
Laid on the ground as the bullets blast
Through glass and doors
Bodies prostrate and parallel to the floor
Lights peering through the curtain
But it's far from morning
And that joy that comes with it
Is hiding in plain sight
It's a cause for celebration
Just to survive the night
Oh hi, please don't be alarmed
If I stare into space or jump
And jitter at the slightest pitter patter
My reflexes have just been bred that way
Some may not understand
I'm not used to many helping hands
And if you're looking for me
I won't be outside playing until
The street lights come on
Or hitting piñatas where all the delicious
Candy comes from
Or even knowing what the delicate flavor
Of innocence tastes like
I'll be here under the covers praying

Until the smoke from the chaos
Clears the atmosphere
Whenever that will be
This isn't the life of a child
They promised me

Wondering Eyes

If I had a million pennies
I would hand them all over
As collateral to reach inside your mind
And freeze a moment in time
You see me alone
Suspended in a daze
Though it's nothing particular
It would be everything to
Know what you're thinking
My eyes have tried to
Penetrate your mental state
Yet, I remain enslaved
To the shackles and chains
That I will make haste to break
And explore your abyss
Reaffirm the real meaning behind
All the body language I may have missed
I don't doubt your convictions
Or think you're telling lies
I just need something secure
To tame these wondering eyes

Get Down To Come Up

Many of you may remember the popular 90s video game Super Mario Bros. The two main characters in the game were Mario and Luigi. I've never been much of a huge gamer (mainly because it's an expensive trend to keep up with), but the Super Mario series of games still remain some of my favorites to this day. When I was younger, I had a Mario action figure that had a spring and a suction cup that could be pushed down. When the spring was pushed all the way down, the suction cup would adhere to the base of the spring; within a few seconds, Mario would leap off of the table. The toy was very simple and I got bored with it rather quickly. Nonetheless it taught me a concept that has stuck with me in my adult life, specifically within the last year.

Just like that toy, we sometimes have to be pushed down in order to spring upward. We can't see it at the time and it just feels like we're being overlooked, overworked, being treated unfairly and being passed up for a better life. At that very moment, that may be true. Life constantly moves in seasons and sometimes it just may be a season where we are leaping forward and everything is going smoothly. However, what goes up, must come down. We all will have our share of bad days and for some it may even feel like more than a fair share of misfortune.

In times like these, the best thing to keep in mind is that often times, the longer we stay low determines the height of our victory. I'm a firm believe that your words and your mindset play a huge part in your circumstances. Maybe this is your "get down" period in life where you are waiting to spring forward into your destiny. That time may be delayed by our own carnal timing. However, keeping a positive outlook about it and knowing that it's only temporary will at least help during those times when the spring hasn't quite popped yet. Your "get down" is only a set up for a "come up".

Breathe

Today my only desire is to breathe
Not just haphazardly filling my
Lungs with air
I want to breathe dammit
It's my right, my demand, my decree
And the only way for me to release
Exhaling the tensions and the toxins
Of the day into the winds to be carried away
I want to breathe like I just climbed the
Top of the mountain
Triumphant and bold and rolling
Beaming even, with purpose
I don't want to be restricted this time
When I breathe
I don't want to hear anyone telling me
My breaths are too loud or not melodic enough
I am going to breathe my own rhythmic patterns
And make music that only
I understand
Do you understand?
I want to swim underneath the currents
And even breathe underwater with no
Man made apparatus
Just because they said I couldn't do it
Just when they begin to doubt
I'll prove it
That my breaths are worth acknowledging
In the same manner theirs are
And anyone that doesn't like it better move

Because the expansion of my breathing
Will fill up the room
Annihilating all gloom and
Cause for doom
I need to breathe

Enabler

When the bow breaks
When the light of the sun
Is just too much to take
When the night sets and settles in
To your utmost fears and insecurities
When running is not feasible
And neither is walking
I will be your crutch
Here to enable you

Behind Bars

Rinse.Wash.Repeat.
Seems that's all we're ever
Good enough to be
Same shit different places
Same people different faces
Walking on two legs
Of redundancy and complacency
We have grown so comfortable
In the mess that should cause
the greatest discomfort
Rinse.Wash.Repeat
Walking zombies with numbed
Sense of self-esteem
We want it all
Yet we want nothing
We want the truth
But lies are what we're loving
Pushing shoving to get nowhere fast
Rebels without a known cause
Rally cries that don't last
Past the change of the second hand
We've had many times over a second chance
But still we Rinse.Wash.Repeat
Dirty filthy me
You'd think after all this cleansing
There would be a little more substance
To see through the grime and the grit
That should be nonexistent
Just me my soap and I
Rinse.Wash.Repeat
No surprises here

This is who I have perpetually proved to be
Every day of the week
In order to break this vicious cycle
The change must start with me

Homesick

We are professional wanderers
Squandering footsteps in 360 degree trails
A nomadic journeys with no idea
Of the pinnacles and pitfalls it entails
Callouses crush the dirt
Beneath us
Looking to the sky for direction, a compass
Yet have the nerve to be pompous
Chest out, no doubt we
Believe we have arrived
And we have
Right back where we started
No more knowledge gained
Than when we first departed
We signal for the nearest
Sign of reprieve
At ease and we were never
Standing at attention
We've somehow lost our way
But did we ever have it to begin with?

Awake

I was awoke
When the faint traces of sunlight
Reminded me of what was ahead
That I couldn't bear to face
I was awoke when I turned on the TV
To watch the news of bullets
Being sprayed profusely across nations
Killing each other with haste and
Feeling claustrophobic even within
My own space and
I was awoke when I felt the
Chilling touch of reality at the
Bottom of my feet
Before I was even able to brush my teeth
I was awoke and a believer of
All the things they said I couldn't do
What they said I couldn't be
Not knowing that it was like acid
Eroding the passion inside of me
I awoke and showered but could
Not wash away the filth of my past and
The joyous declarations of what I was
Sure to come from their lips as they whispered
"See, I knew he couldn't do it"
But then one day I woke up
Awakened to the world outside my window that
I never knew
Red robins and branches and blue jays on fences
Urged me to join them atop the morning dew
In all their marvelous hues
My mountains became just monumental mounds of dirt

That I could actually climb over
My valleys become launching pads to propel me to the sky
I overcame my deepest fears and set the blueprint
For all others to follow
I AM AWAKE

I Heard About You

There's something about me that makes many people feel comfortable to spill out their dark secrets to me. I like to think of it as a compliment because I take other people's business very seriously. I get no joy in spreading intimate details about someone else's business to the general public or at times even other people I'm close to. I have found it to be quite comical when I hear people nod at something they heard about me through someone else.

Although I do care about what people I love think about me, I could care less what associates and strangers think of me. People's opinions always change and sometimes it's best to just take what is said about you with a grain of salt. Loyalty is one of the pillars of any kind of relationship. Often times, people can feel too common and think they can say anything on their mind. If I'm close to someone, I make it known that no one should feel comfortable enough to say certain things about someone I'm close to.

People who are always willing to tell what they heard about someone else are not only being talked about (as we all are), but they also will tell anything. There is a word on the street about everyone, depending on what street you're on. I don't know what about the human race makes them feel superior to others because of what they think they know.

So many people spend their entire existence concerned about what other people think of them. Does it really matter? If we know who we are, what we stand for and who we stand for, we shouldn't be so worried concerned with opinions that fail to pay bills for us or put food on our table.

Incapable

My love is not preemptive
Nor does it wither and waver towards
The highest bidder
Because the odds are with the house
My love is not something you can
Catapult high and look low upon
Like an elf on a shelf
I'd rather just
Leave that to somebody else
Because my love just.....is
My love is quite simple
Not a complicated quandry
To be decoded
It is letting me think I'm right
Every now and then
Even if I'm damn wrong
It's bubble baths and tears with laughs
It's rubbing my bald head
But not immediately after I've shaved
It's the quirky idiosyncrasies
Without one word ever having to be whispered
And even better, no judgment for it
It's remembering my favorite piece of candy
It's taking time to smell the roses
Even when things arent so fine and dandy
It's being my one avenger
When the whole world stands as a contender
To try to tear me down
You wouldn't stand for that would you?
My love is at times like vinegar's sting
That will test your tolerance to taste

My love may be many things
Some sour, some delectable
But being artificial is one thing
It is totally incapable of

Green Fiends

We are green fiends
In pursuit of plush dreams
Fast cars and shiny things
What green can help you achieve
Some get so engulfed in it
That they barely even sleep
Green can mask your presence
To the world
Give your pain a different hue
But does green really matter
When inside you're black and blue?
All the green you can hold
Still we can't escape the truth
We will kill, steal and lie
To have that green by our side
Unapolegtic hunters
If you look closely
Beneath the disguise
It comes as no surprise
That you can start to see
The green in our eyes
But when we leave the green stays
To its power were the slaves
Who will remember what you did
Remember what you said
How much does the green really matter
If we all bleed red?

My Current Situation

Good morning
The skies are pitch black
As the stars have retreated
Behind the dimly lit moonlight
This is no good night
Choppy waters flush against
The unstable raft
There is not much
Strength left to push
To what instinctly feels like the shore
Wait, quiet
There's something moving in the water
Maybe they can smell the blood
From my bumps and bruises
Hopefully they won't find me, hungry
Here I am forced to face me totally
No mirror could reflect any clearer
As I settle in to direct my thoughts
On the rising of the sun
Not my current situation of
Tumultuous tides that rise
Way beyond my eyes
Wise navigation won't steer me wrong
Good morning
This night won't last too long

Glutinous Monster

Everyone else could see you
From the inside out
I saw it too but chose to
Take your insides out
And hang them out to dry until
Every flaw drip dropped
Rough and gritty
Mesmerized and somehow
Your ugly became pretty
A beast to many
But you provided a sense
Of Protection
Direction
Reflection is a bit late
Because it's not so easy to peel away
At this particular juncture
I ignored every puncture of my sanity
Telling me to escape what had become
My new reality
Glutinous, sticky
Not to be confused with
Gluttonous, really
Though I did that too
Couldn't get enough of you
And I became greedy and
Ravenous behind a slow, sweet poison
Leaving me nothing more
Than a listless testimony
Of what not to do
Truly stuck like glue

Bed Warmer

She did whatever she could
To hold on for dear life
Wiped the blood from her knuckles
Swept the dust off her knees
That were used to the position of
Pleading and pleasing
Yet to no avail
She washed her hair with
Rainwater and spun around 7 times
Thinking that the sun would somehow
Rise upon his heart to then take hers
The sun has risen 1,756 times since then
Her bed stays cold and lonely
Only knowing warmth on the nights
When he's in between her thighs
Grinding and moaning promises in her ear
It was always how she knew when the climax was near
They were sweet lies that kept
Her strung along like
The stepping of untied shoe laces
Underneath quickly moving feet
Stumbling over her dignity
But she needs him
She craves him
She wants him
Can't you understand?
Haven't you been there before?
Wasn't there something you yearned
For so deeply that you would sacrifice
Your own good sense to seize it?
Then perhaps you can relate to why

She feels the need to perpetually degrade
Herself for him
For he who has yet to even
Notice her soul is slowly slipping away
He does still keep her bed warm from
Time to time though
For her, that must be enough

Kissy Face

Kissy face, honey dip
Sugar lump
Waves on the love ship
Shared with the world
Until it implodes
And everybody knows
The consequence of kissy faces
Unkept behind closed doors

When The Dam Breaks

I have never actually witnessed a dam breaking. However, I can imagine it would be a pretty frightening experience. Obviously the barrier was there for a reason and the force of all of the water rushing in at one instant could cause some serious damage. There have been several times in life where I've felt like I was in the midst of a dam breaking experience.

At that moment, there wasn't much I could do to prevent it. The mess had already commenced and it was beyond my realm of control for containing. Granted, in most situations, a damn breaking is never a good thing. There are some times where we need the dam to break though in order to be carried to a place that's better for us.

The rituals of habit are dangerous because over time they create a complacent spirit within us. Often times, it takes what seems like a disaster to get our attention. The dam breaking is just what we needed to stop leaning on our own understanding and solely depend on God. Have you ever noticed that when everything is going well in life, you actually pray less?

Maybe I'm telling on myself, but trials bring us back into a dependent state where we have to acknowledge we're in above our heads. In 2016, there were some moments like this for me where I felt like everything was breaking beyond my control. Let's face it, no one likes to be in a situation that is uncontrollable.

The dam breaking can be that rapid cleanse we need to wash away the doubt, fear, anxiety and complacency that we were clinging so strongly to. At the time, we can't see where the waters are taking us until we finally reach the shore on the other side. We can't pinpoint the exact time of when the dam will break. The best thing for us to do is learn during the process and pay attention to those things we are supposed to carry away as lessons once we reach the other side. A dam breaking moment is just an abrupt set up for something greater. Let the waters lead you where you need to be.

Whispers

If you're quiet you can
Barely hear their utterances
Warning me of damp, sticky
Corridors detrimental to me
Now silent whispers in the dark
Become blaring scream in the light
A Truth so bright it leaves us blind
And void of the strength to squelch

Marked Up

By the time I finally came to
There were 96 stab wounds
Painful lacerations
Due to no probably cause or confrontation
Some belonged to others
And some had my name
Written all over them
In crimson, listen
To the screams of agony
As the scars that no one
Can see begin to form
Some of the cuts were made
When some of them were born
Some were made as a result of loving
Too hard or not enough
Some were self-inflicted
Like walking barefoot on a bed
Jagged and jarred glass
You know before you took
Another step it was bound to
Cut your ass
Didn't you?
The assailants are long gone from sight
Yet so near and clear in view
We have survived what was designed
To cripple us
Mangle us
Destroy us
Suffocate us
Obliterate us

By the time we finally came to
We realized all of these cuts, scars and bruises
Were just testaments of how we made it through

If These Chairs Could Talk

Have you ever wondered
What the chair thinks?
How the chair feels?
After some of us have
Left its presence
That's if we ever do
I imagine it would say
Something like this

These legs were never
Meant to hold you up forever
Yet you sit here day after day
Month after month
Year after year
Professing pointless resolutions
Go figure, I'm ruined

Over time I have evolved
To give you more spinal support
Improve your posture to just
Make more excuses
And cushion to make your
Complacency more comfortable
I no longer recognize myself
Or my worth until you take your seat

But there is a bright side to
All of this
I have evolved, yet
You have remained stagnant
In fact rolling backwards

Like those smiley face
Price cuts at WalMart
Into an ignorant abyss
What's your worth now?
About a dollar and fifty six cents?

These legs have grown weary
And plead for you to one day
Some way, get off your ass
And make something of yourself
My existence is eroded
Nothing more than a mere excuse
To make your comfort zone
A lazy, nondescript throne

It's Gonna Burn

We knew the danger of the heat before
We touched it
Yet we knew not just how detrimental
Those yellow, orange, purple, blue and red hues
Could be until we
Hovered our hands barely over the tip
Of the flames, oops
Maybe I should remove the we
And insert me
Maybe I'm the only one
But somehow having a partner in crime
Makes us or should I say me feel
Less guilty
And now it burns
Now it pangs
Now it stings
Open up the windows
To air out the screams
And hear them ring
As the temperature of the blood
Rushing through our veins rises
From the spectacular mess we've made
Until it becomes a strange addiction
We learn to crave
I could trade my existence with you
But chances are you've had your share
Of over, under and through
The flame experiences too
We know it hurts

We know there are
Irreversible repercussions
So why is it again that we
Can't help but touch it?

Sniff

Their snouts brush against your toes
You back away and call it gross
But he knows you'll fall every time
For these pleading, puppy dog eyes
He said fetch, you caught his bone
And now he calls your place his home
Late night creeping through
The doggie door
Marking his territory by figuratively
Pissing on your floor
To let them know you're his
While he's out with Monica, Tina and Liz
But you just giggle and say it's cute
After all, a man without a temper
Really doesn't love you
Then you finally kicked him out
Dirty paws and that wet snout
You wave your hands
And join the parade
Oh, you're a real single lady now
And if he was serious, your love
He would have saved
But this one thing
You perpetually miss
If it didn't fit, you must acquit
If you didn't have such a desperate stench
Maybe he wouldn't have had reason to sniff
Maybe he would have been the one to commit

Quicksand (Don't Pull Me Out)

I remember just like it was yesterday
When I first dipped my toe
Into this forbidden sand
One foot in now and
The other is barely planted on dry land
Until before I knew it
I was slowly slipping in
Curiosity won over my fear
And sinking was merely a means
For me to fall deeper into
Being swallowed whole
Which I didn't mind
After a while I didn't care
That the sand was in my eyes
I adapted and learned how to
Breathe beneath the surface of
Reality because this experience became
So breathtaking to me
That I began to recruit others
To dive in with me
Into this fantasy of an abyss
Ain't that some ….
I made my own comfortable bed
And this is where I'll lay
I know I can't survive like this forever
But for now, this is where I'll stay

Keep Digging If You Want To

One of the qualities I thought was really cool about stingrays when I researched them for this book is how calm they are. These are animals that basically mind their own business and really only attack when they are being threatened. I consider myself to have a kindred spirit to many of the stingrays. I would be rich if I had one dollar every time someone told me how nice I am. People that just know me on the surface (and even a few that know me well) think that I'm never angry or upset about anything. This is the furthest thing from the truth. I get ticked off just like the next person, but I believe it's all about how you handle it.

One of my pet peeves though is when people try to push my temper or pull anger out of me. There is a chance you have heard these words as well, "I wonder what really makes you mad". I just laugh to myself and think, "Keep pushing me and you'll find out". I wouldn't call myself a ticking time bomb but I can let many things roll of my back without holding grudges. Ok, I'm human. Maybe I have held a grudge or two before in the past, but not lately.

When a person that is perceived as mean gives someone a piece of their mind, no one flinches. People expect it. They just get out of the way and basically let them unleash their wrath. However, when a perceived quiet person does the same thing, it's the end of the world.

Unfortunately, there will always be someone to push your buttons. One thing I've learned with time is it's better to nip certain things in the bud just for principal (even if it doesn't greatly bother you). By the time we mention things at the point of anger, we run a greater risk of being irrational, saying/doing things we don't mean and even causing physical harm to ourselves (stress). Be calm. Be cool. Be like the stingray, but don't wait until people back you into a corner before you tell them how you really feel.

You Get What You Don't Ask For

I'm by no means a relationship expert, but there's one motto when it comes to dating that I've always lived by. Actually, I believe this principal even transcends being in a relationship. As a society, we are encouraged to speak up for what we want in life. I do agree with this principal for the most part, but there are times when we need to make our requests known and leave it at that. I've never been one to succumb to pressure to do something just because someone asks me to repeatedly.

Ladies, some of you may disagree, but it's a little like hitting a button to wait for the elevator. Many times, I've seen people hit the button several times, hoping that will make it arrive quicker. I'll admit, I used to do it a few times too when I was younger. Note that I said when I was younger. Hint, hint, at some point we should put childish things aside. Yet, I digress.

Let's go ahead and attack the elephant in the room and relate this to marriage. I actually know several women who have told their boyfriends at the time that if they got engaged, their ring had to be a certain size. Yes, I nearly flipped my lid too when I heard it. Who does this? Sadly, so many women do.

Don't get me wrong. Everyone should make it known what they want in life, but there's a way to do it that's nonabrasive. In these types of scenarios, one of two things will happen. Either the woman gets exactly what she wants or the man purposely doesn't give it to her as a direct result of voicing her desires one too many times (pushing that elevator button again).

Maybe the guy was preparing to get a 3 carat engagement ring, but you demanded that it be at least 2 carats. Trust me, he's likely going to choose the latter instead. Maybe he wants to give you the world but simply doesn't have the budget. Then some wonder why he later gives it to the one who kept her mouth closed when he gains more money. Here's the painful kicker. Perhaps the guy decides to just cut all ties simply because he was constantly being nagged. Scary thought isn't it?

Remember this. Ask if you must but realize that it won't compare to the satisfaction of being surprised by it instead. Some things really are better left unsaid.

Seashells

Just beneath the ocean's floor
I can feel them underneath my feet
Between my toes as they wash up
Gently along the shore
Sometimes I envy them
And their ability to disappear
Reemerging only when they
Are ready to be kissed by the sun
In the stills of the night they
Float past each other
Sharp edges colliding
Rolling in the deep of the waves
That encompass them
They are no respectors of persons
Creeds, genders or races
And are found in the most unsuspecting places
Their ears bent to the sky
Absorbing the surroundings
Of all the passersby.....

Freedom To Think (Don't Speak)

2016 was a year filled with tragedy that didn't discriminate against its targets of hate crimes and attacks. Various races, religious groups and sexual orientations were targeted. There was virtually no stone left unturned and honestly I felt like it made everyone on edge to even carry out some of their daily tasks. Then comes social media.

The presence and accessibility of social media can turn a regular civilian into a news reporter just from streaming live or posting photos before the news stations even have a chance too. There are two sides of this coin that are definitely worth discussing. On one hand, online activity in regards to crime may help police catch suspects quicker or seal the deal for justice for those who physically weren't at the scene of the crime.

During sensitive times like these, the first place many people flock to is Facebook, Twitter, Instagram, Periscope and whatever other social media outlet they can get to the quickest. Don't get me wrong, we should all be able to express our freedom of speech. Some people even say that those who remain silent are part of the problem.

However, I beg to differ. The issue with everyone exercising their freedom of speech is some people should just really shut up if they have nothing intelligent or enlightening to add to the discussion. When it comes to influence, there have even been celebrities and government officials who have made statements on social media that only fuel more hate, not bring us together.

Then there are the attention whores. Yep, those people who can't wait to use the latest trending hashtag of someone who was violently killed or so called supporting for a city's catastrophic disaster. There are those who have a voice that enhances the conversation and have influence to actually initiate positive change.

I won't mention the actual incident here, but last year I remember seeing a meme someone created of them dressed up in a suit with a caption that read, "I Don't Want To Be A Hashtag". The actual hashtags included in their post were #toetag, #bodybag and the names of some of the victims during that time period. Looking at their previous posts (which had no substance whatsoever), it's hard to take people like that seriously. Whether we want to believe it or not, social media has created cowards and impressionable generations.

Let's all be mindful of what we're saying and how we say it on social media. Yes, we do have the right to freedom of speech. However, there are more times than not when some of us should use our right to remain silent.

Make Me A Believer

Honestly, I don't need your truths
You can plead your case of how
Transparent they are like
Overhead projectors in grade school
You can even lie to me
Straight to my face
Look me in my eyes
Without your breathing pattern
Making any hiccup or haste
Or your heartbeat failing to speed up its pace
Just make me a believer
Really, that's all I ask
And let the burden of proof
Rest as heavily as smothering boulders
Or as lightly as delicate feathers
On your shoulders
It's on you, literally
And what weight you are comfortable
Carrying around as the moon chases the sun
In 360 degrees of perfectly balanced chaos
I don't have the mental capacity
To accuse you of having the audacity
To lie, to me
Because if you button it up
Well enough, no one can peel back
The layers to peak at
What's underneath

Make my perception create the
Mold of my reality of you
That no one can shake my faith from
Give me no doubts, second thoughts
Butterflies or intuitions
That's really, truly all I'll ever ask for

Proof In The Negatives

We spend so much time
Hiding away quietly in darkness
We forget how it feels for
Light exposure to dance upon our skin
There is beauty in the flaws
And yet we erase them all
In the name of coming to slay
Or so we say
Making every excuse under the sun
But afraid to live under its microscope
Like vampires sucking the life out of
Ourselves all for the sake
Of someone else's approval
That won't give more than a
Mere like, share or retweet
That can't be redeemed to buy any groceries
That can't be redeemed when more than social
Acceptance is needed to get through the night
That can't be redeemed when the darkness seems to smother the light
So we try with all our might to edit the negatives
Before they are fully developed
Ignoring the fact that there's
Promise in the negatives
There's purpose in the negatives
We distort our souls whose torture
Eventually surfaces on our faces
And all other visible places
We have destroyed the negatives beyond recognition
With no proof of what and who they contained

Skin Deep

You are in love with
The perception of me
Not fully understanding
Depth of me
The surface me
Is what you see
Intoxicated inside a revelry
But what would you think
If you peeled back these layers
Bit down harder until you
Tasted all the icky flavors
Maybe I should do you a favor
And stop you while you're ahead
Can you shuffle through my organized noise?
Are you strong enough to hold
What you've requested for so long
And now you have it
Unhappily harboring the ill feelings
Of the truth behind inquiries
You really didn't want to
Know the answer to
They say that beauty is only skin deep
Well your love is too
If I can't uncover my ugly with you
Do you still love me now
Now that I'm stripped in front of you

Tangible Lucidness

I remember tangible lucidness
Yet it all seems so far
Out of my grasp now
My fingertips graze
The very threads
Of its coattails
Quiet
Be ever so still
And you can hear it
Whisking away in the night
I remember tangible lucidness
During a time when
Conversational tones
Were not muddled with
Misread nonverbal cues
When love was something
That could be tasted, smelled and touched
Not floating around a virtual reality space
Yes, I do recall tangible lucidness
Don't you?
I can still think of a time when
Having less was more
And having more was useless
I could use a lucid dream or two fulfilled
Couldn't you?

Smile In The Sky

Though I'll never get to share
The same space and glow
Of your physical presence
That illuminates a room
I have the memories of
Your sprit that spoke without speaking
Which help me get through
Those moments of gloom
I know that it may seem selfish of me
To believe that such a
Selfless anomaly like yourself
Would always be around to
Give the warmest, most sincere smile
This side of heaven has ever felt
Instead of perpetually weeping
We will graciously play this
Surviving hand we have been dealt
As your aura is felt like
A bionic force field protecting us
Guiding us through its bubble in the atmosphere
And when the pang of pain
Jabs us unexpectedly
We will look up and find that
Same warm smile so high
Beaming with revelry
Dancing with freedom
Shouting with an unparalleled joy
Ah, yes that same warm smile
Is no longer tied to these earthly troubles
Its new mission is to ignite like fireworks
And light up the sky

Coming Later This Year…..

No Cream In The Middle, the follow up to *Fortune Cookie*.

You won't believe the secrets Cookie and her sister are hiding this time.

His mortality flashed before his eyes on his way down. There didn't seem to be any time to think between when the SUV mashed into the barricade several times and him being ultimately ejected from the vehicle. All he knew was this was not how his life was supposed to end. If he ever had the chance, he would seek revenge by taking matters into his own hands. He would make sure they both suffered long, slow deaths. But as he accelerated towards the water, his plan seemed doomed; and so did his life.

Boom! His body slapped the surface of the water as large shards of glass grazed across his skin. As he plunged into the water, he could tell he had been cut from the pain of the wounds. His chest and back immediately felt sore from the forceful impact of falling from the bridge and into the water. Despite his pain and fatigue, the adrenaline of the moment helped him push his way back to the surface of the water. The surrounding areas were pitch black and he could barely even see any stars. He could look up and see the road lights on the bridge, but they were of no help to him down here.

That's when everything went black and it wasn't just from the darkness outside. He could still comprehend everything that was happening but his body was paralyzed. He didn't see a way out of this one and his energy was quickly waning. He must have been losing consciousness. There was nothing he could do now but accept his fate.

After what seemed like an eternity, he finally found some semblance of dry land. There was a faint light looming over his head. It was just before dawn. When he finally came to, he could faintly make out a woman kneeling over him. Her hands were moving towards his chest and she looked just like Cookie. Was it her coming to finish him off? He wasn't going to let that happen.

With a jolt of energy resembling an electric shock, he reached out and began choking her. He squeezed harder and harder as Cookie kicked, screamed and shouted to break free. That's when he got a really close look. It wasn't Cookie after all. Just a woman that looked eerily similar to her. He then loosened the grip on her neck.

The woman hacked up from the back of her throat and spit in his face and then slapped him. "How dare you?! You crazy bastard! I found you out here and was just trying to see if you were still alive," the woman screamed. Brandon apologized, but she was too far gone and frazzled at this point. Still coughing and gasping for air, she decided to call the police.

"Wait. Wait! I'm very sorry. There's no need to do that. I'm Jason by the way. I just thought you were someone else. I got into a horrible accident last night. I know it sounds crazy, but I'd rather not get the police involved. Nothing they can really do now anyway at this point, you know," he said.

"I understand. Well, I probably should go then. I hope you find the help you need," the woman responded. She was clearly out for a morning run, judging by her attire. Ironically, there weren't any other people out around them. As Brandon stood up, he did see a man far in the distance. He just wasn't sure if he was heading their way. "You know you really look like you need some medical attention. Let me at least call and get you some help, ok?"

Brandon stared at her as he watched her dial 911. He couldn't believe that she completely disobeyed his command. He had to think quickly, while there was still no one around them. He slammed the phone to the ground with one hand and grabbed the back of her head with the other. He dragged her by her hair until they reached the edge of the water again. Brandon held her underneath the shallow water just long enough for her to stop breathing. Once she became as limp as a ragdoll, he whispered softly in her ear, "Maybe next time when I tell you to do something, you'll just follow instructions".

About The Author

Carlos Harleaux is a poet, author and CEO of 7th Sign Publishing. His previous literary works include three poetry books (*Blurred Vision*, *Hindsight 20/20* and *Honesty Box*) and one novel (*Fortune Cookie*). Carlos also holds a Masters in Emerging Media and Communication. He is an avid blogger, discussing various topics including music, inspiration and writing from an author's perspective. Carlos is originally from Houston, TX and currently resides in Dallas, TX with his wife, Alex.

www.ingramcontent.com/pod-product-compliance
Lightning Source LLC
Chambersburg PA
CBHW051954290426
44110CB00015B/2235